AMERICA'S ARMED FORCES

The U.S. HOMELAND SECURITY FORCES

HUNTER KEETER

WORLD ALMANAC® LIBRARY

Please visit our web site at: **www.worldalmanaclibrary.com**
For a free color catalog describing World Almanac® Library's list of high-quality books
and multimedia programs, call 1-800-848-2928 (USA) or 1-800-387-3178 (Canada).
World Almanac® Library's fax: (414) 332-3567.

Library of Congress Cataloging-in-Publication Data

Keeter, Hunter.
    The U.S. Homeland Security forces / by Hunter Keeter.
      p. cm. — (America's armed forces)
    Includes bibliographical references and index.
    ISBN 0-8368-5682-1 (lib. bdg.)
    ISBN 0-8368-5689-9 (softcover)
    1. Civil defense—United States—Juvenile literature. 2. National security—
United States—Juvenile literature. 3. War on Terrorism, 2001—Juvenile literature.
4. United States—Defenses—Juvenile literature. I. Title: United States Homeland
Security forces. II. United States. Dept. of Homeland Security. III. Title. IV. Series.
UA927.K39   2004
363.35'0973—dc22
                                    2004042793

First published in 2005 by
World Almanac® Library
330 West Olive Street, Suite 100
Milwaukee, WI 53212 USA

Copyright © 2005 by World Almanac® Library.

Developed by Amber Books Ltd.
Editor: James Bennett
Designer: Colin Hawes
Photo research: Sandra Assersohn, Natasha Jones
World Almanac® Library editor: Mark Sachner
World Almanac® Library art direction: Tammy West
World Almanac® Library production: Jessica Morris

Picture Acknowledgements
Corbis: 4, 5, 6, 8, 9 (both), 25, 26, 27; U.S.DoD.: 7, 10, 18, 19, 29, 31, 35, 36, 38, 39, 40,
41, 43; F.E.M.A: 11, 22, 28, 35; N.O.R.A.D: 34; U.S. Coast Guard: 12, 13, 14, 15, 16, 20, 21;
TRH: 24; Topham Picturepoint: cover, 32.

Printed in Canada

1 2 3 4 5 6 7 8 9 08 07 06 05 04

About the Author

HUNTER KEETER is a journalist with *Defense Daily*, a leading defense business
publication. On September 11, 2001, he was at his desk in the Pentagon press room
during the terrorist attacks. While reporting on the ensuing war against global terrorism
he developed a detailed knowledge of the missions and responsibilities of the
Department of Homeland Security. He lives in Arlington, Virginia.

Table of Contents

Right: On September 11, 2001, a terrorist attack destroyed New York City's World Trade Center. In this photograph, a U.S. Coast Guard boat patrols New York Harbor near the site of the ruined twin towers.

After 19 hijackers on September 11, 2001, used commercial airliners as weapons to kill an estimated 2,795 people in New York City, 44 at Shanksville, Pennsylvania, and 189 at the Pentagon near Washington, D.C., the United States government decided that responding to and recovering from future attacks would require more centralized organization. To achieve this, the government created a new office, the Department of Homeland Security, reporting directly to the White House. The new department comprised agencies that had been part of other government departments, such as the U.S. Coast Guard, and law enforcement organizations, such as the U.S. Secret Service and the U.S. Customs Service, as well as the Federal Emergency Management Agency (FEMA), among others.

The Coast Guard is the only military force directly under the management of the Department of Homeland Security. The Department of Defense controls the U.S. Army, U.S. Navy, U.S. Marine Corps, and U.S. Air Force, which take the lion's share in America's defense operations. The Department of Defense, working with 59 state and territorial governments, also administers reserve forces, including the U.S. Army National Guard and the U.S. Air Force Air National Guard, both of which make significant contributions to homeland defense.

Law enforcement agencies outside the Department of Homeland Security also help promote internal security. Agencies such as the Federal Bureau of Investigation (FBI) and the Drug Enforcement Agency (DEA), both of which are part of the U.S. Department of Justice, are responsible for detecting and preventing criminal acts (such as terrorist attacks) and other types of crimes. Federal law enforcement agencies in the United States contribute to the government's intelligence network as well, predicting potential threats to national security. For example, the investigations of the FBI, the DEA, and the Department of Homeland Security's own Secret Service produce valuable information about the nature and location of terrorist groups, spies, and saboteurs.

Below: Soldiers of the U.S. Army National Guard have assumed a more public role since 2001, helping police and other forces enhance security at airports, border crossings, and other high-traffic areas.

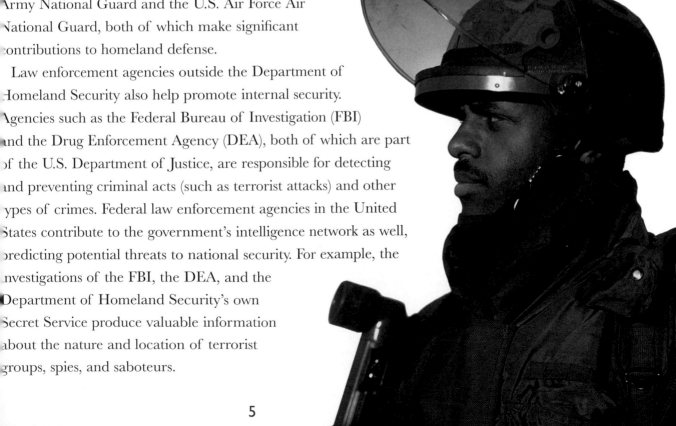

Chapter 1
Threats and Responses

Right: A helicopter patrols overhead as the Pentagon burns, September 11, 2001. Terrorists crashed a hijacked Boeing 757 airliner into the U.S. military headquarters.

Operation Enduring Freedom, which began with the 2001–2002 war in Afghanistan and now continues with other efforts, became the first high-profile blow struck in response to the September 11, 2001, terrorist attacks. The United States and its allies—including Australia, Canada, Denmark, France, Germany, and Great Britain—launched a campaign to dismantle the government of the Taliban in Afghanistan, which supported terrorist activity by hosting the al-Qaeda network.

The Taliban was formed in 1994, initially as a militia group to combat human rights abuses by Afghanistan's warring factions following the overthrow of a Soviet-backed government. The Taliban by 1996 had assumed power in Afghanistan, replacing the former regime with a religious government that was characterized by a strict form of Islam that limited or erased the rights of women and those of some traditional Afghan minority cultures.

In *Resolution 1390*, which was endorsed by the United Nations Security Council in 2002, the Taliban regime was condemned for having allowed Afghanistan to be used as a base for terrorist training and operations, "including the export of terrorism by al-Qaeda and other groups." The form of Islam practiced by the Taliban government shared some basic beliefs with groups like al-Qaeda. Given the rural and undeveloped nature of the Afghan countryside, al-Qaeda found in Afghanistan a friendly and ready-made refuge within which to train its operatives and carry out plans for attacks such as those of September 11, 2001.

Operation Enduring Freedom now encompasses the less public actions of special operations forces and other nations' militaries and police forces. On April 1, 2003, a report to Congress noted that U.S. military units were working with other nations' law enforcement and military agencies to hunt al-Qaeda

Below: Operation Enduring Freedom, the battle to oust the Taliban government from Afghanistan, included U.S. Navy F/A-18 Hornet strike fighters flying from aircraft carriers in the Arabian Sea.

and its allied terrorist organizations, including the Islamic Movement of Uzbekistan, Jemaah Islamiyah in Indonesia, and Abu Sayyaf in the Philippines. The United States provides money, training programs, weapons, and equipment to allied nations' forces fighting against the spread of global terrorism.

Terrorism is not a new problem. The world has experience dealing with the economic, political, and social consequences of terrorism, such as bombings, **assassinations**, and kidnappings. In the Americas, political violence became a serious problem during the 1960s, 1970s, and 1980s. In Northern Ireland, in Spain, and in Germany, politically and culturally motivated violence has also jeopardized security. In the Middle East and in Africa, fighting between different ideologies, religions, and cultures became ferocious after World War II (1939–194[5] and the founding of the modern state of Israel. Asian nations have also struggled against the spread of violence. In the view of many government leaders, perhaps second only to public health crises such as the global spread of HIV/AIDS, terrorism poses a significant threat to safety, social stability, and prosperity.

Determined Adversaries

The development of well-funded and, in some cases, state-supported, global networks of terrorists capable of organizing and carrying out attacks such as those of September 11, 2001, is fairly recent, however. One such well-organized group, the Islamic **fundamentalists** known as al-Qaeda—which means "the movement" or "the base" in Arabic—is believed to have been responsible for the September 11 attacks, as well as a number of other terror incidents in the 1990s and early part of the twenty-first century. al-Qaeda is exemplary because it is a characteristically shadowy association of smaller groups whose ideologies and goals are similar.

According to a Department of State intelligence report from 2002, Saudi Arabian millionaire Osama bin Laden established al-Qaeda during the 1980s to support Islamic fighters who had resisted the Soviet Union's presence in Afghanistan. The Soviet Union sent a large military force into Afghanistan in the late 1970s in order to support the government against **nationalist** resistance. In 2001, al-Qaeda merged with an Egyptian group called al-Jihad to

Below: Osama bin Laden, Saudi-Arabian-born leader of al-Qaeda, has called for Muslims to rise in violence against the United States and its allies around the world.

8

Left: In 2001, the U.S. military established a prison at Naval Base Guantanamo Bay, Cuba, to house suspected terrorists captured in Afghanistan and elsewhere.

orm what is today one of the world's most widespread organizations advocating he use of politically and religiously motivated violence. al-Qaeda's goal, ccording to the State Department's report, is to:

*"Establish a pan-Islamic **caliphate** throughout the world by working with allied Islamic xtremist groups to overthrow regimes it deems non-Islamic and expelling Westerners and non-Muslims from Muslim countries, particularly Saudi Arabia. al-Qaeda issued a statement…in ebruary 1998, saying it was the duty of all Muslims to kill U.S. citizens, civilian or military, nd their allies everywhere."*

Below left: Pennsylvania Representative Curt R. Weldon displays a mock-up of a so-called "suitcase nuke." Some government officials believe such devices — small nuclear bombs disguised as luggage — could be used by terrorists.

Nuclear Fear

During the height of the Cold War, in the 1950s and the 1960s, there was a very real possibility that nuclear war could occur. During that period of history, events such as the 1962 Cuban Missile Crisis, where Soviet nuclear weapons were discovered at bases in Cuba, just 90 miles from the United States, made civil authorities prepare for the worst. Many people built bomb blast and radiation shelters near their homes.

Above: U.S. President George W. Bush greets Army National Guardsmen at the Pentagon on September 16, 2001.

Raising the Stakes

One of the most frightening threats posed by international terrorism is the possibility of the use of weapons of mass destruction (nuclear, biological, chemical, or radiological devices—also known as WMD) to create large numbers of casualties. The threat posed by the possible use of WMD has raised the stakes for defense against modern acts of terrorism, which may one day be capable of causing casualties numbering in the millions rather than the thousands. As evidence emerges of the growing availability of such weapons technology, the U.S. government is working with allies around the world to limit and track the sale of technologies that could be used to spread weapons of mass destruction.

After World War II ended, the conflict between capitalism (an economic system that embraces profit-making and a worldwide free market) and communism (an economic and political ideology that embraces collective ownership of resources and a state-directed labor force) was the source of international fears of war, invasion, espionage, and other threats. Successive administrations in the United States and other nations opposed communism during the Cold War (1945–1991). The Cold War got its name from the fact that tensions between the West and the Soviet Bloc came to the brink of war without openly acknowledged fighting taking place. In the final months of World War II, the United States had become the first and, to date, only nation to employ atomic weapons in combat with the bombing of the Japanese cities of Hiroshima and Nagasaki. When the Soviet Union demonstrated that it, too, possessed atomic weapons, in August 1949, a nuclear arms race was on. Both nations attempted to gain technological advantage over the weapons believed to be in the possession of their rival. All-out nuclear war became a real possibility.

The technologies that lay at the heart of the Cold War era's threats of war and global annihilation are now becoming more widespread. The physical and engineering theories necessary for developing WMD, while remaining complex, have become more accessible because of increased global access to information (through the Internet and other means) and illegal sales of old, but still dangerous, technology and equipment through the world's arms trade.

Facing the challenges posed by terrorism and the possible use of WMD, the Department of Homeland Security has launched a far-reaching program called "Operation Liberty Shield," under which improvements are being made to transportation and border security. Liberty Shield includes more coastal patrols, escort missions, and inspections to intercept dangerous cargo and terrorist groups' operatives before they can reach the United States. Also, improvements are being made to the computer tracking and data management systems used to monitor air traffic over the United States. An intensive effort is underway by the Department of Homeland Security, the Department of Justice, the Department of Defense, and the Central Intelligence Agency to collect information on and to disrupt potential threats to U.S. security. Security forces and defensive technologies (such as electronic monitoring and encryption systems) are being strengthened at key national **infrastructure** facilities, including chemical plants, fuel refineries, and nuclear power stations. Finally, federal, state, and local crisis-response teams, such as fire departments, police, and emergency medical technicians, are being trained and equipped to better respond in the event of a terrorist attack, especially those involving the use of chemical, biological, or radiological weapons.

Below: Tom Ridge (left), first Secretary of Homeland Security.

A New Cabinet Post

Former Pennsylvania Governor Tom Ridge became the first Secretary of Homeland Security —and a member of the president's cabinet— when the Department of Homeland Security was officially established in January 2002. The Cabinet is a group of offices that helps the president make decisions. The group incorporates the vice president, the Attorney General, and the heads of executive departments, including the departments of Agriculture, Commerce, Defense, Education, Energy, Health and Human Services, Homeland Security, Housing and Urban Development, Interior, Labor, State, Transportation, Treasury, and Veterans Affairs.

Right: The U.S. Coast Guard cutter *Mellon* patrols off Alaska. The Coast Guard has increased patrols and inspections in commercial shipping lanes approaching the United States.

An important part of the United States' homeland defense force is the Coast Guard. A military service of 39,000 active-duty members, the Coast Guard marks its origin to the year 1790, when Congress authorized a fleet of 10 cutters, small ships used to enforce customs duties and other seaborne trade regulations. The Coast Guard has evolved into a military force that maintains a diverse fleet and more than 200 aircraft to perform its missions.

The missions of the modern Coast Guard include military, rescue, and law enforcement functions, such as maritime safety and security, and the protection of the nation's fisheries and other natural resources. According to a collection of Coast Guard statistics for the years 2002 and 2003, the Coast Guard accounts for a daily tally of 10 lives saved, 109 search and rescue operations, $9.6 million worth of illegal drugs seized, and the conduct of 19 maritime-security boarding operations. The capture of **contraband** cargo, such as illegal drugs, may contribute to homeland security by preventing terrorists from using these cargoes to raise money for their attacks, according to the U.S. government.

Coast Guard Tasks

The tasks of the Coast Guard during peacetime include enforcement of regulations on marine traffic, which carries 95 percent of the United States' foreign trade; patrolling 3.4 million square miles of ocean in **territorial waters** and more than 95,000 miles of coastline; and protecting 361 major national ports.

The modern Coast Guard is unique among U.S. military forces in that it has responsibilities in both homeland security and homeland defense. At home, the Coast Guard is a powerful law enforcement organization, inspecting vessels for illegal cargo — such as narcotics and weapons — and undocumented migrants. Overseas, the Coast Guard works with the U.S. Navy and other military forces as was the case during Operation Iraqi Freedom in 2003, when Coast Guard patrol boats in the Arabian Gulf helped capture and hold Iraqi oil distribution platforms.

After September 11, 2001, the government viewed the

Below: The U.S. Coast Guard's fleet includes small boats designed for patrolling New York Harbor and other key ports of entry into the United States.

Above: A boarding party from the U.S. Coast Guard cutter *Jarvis* discovers undocumented Asian migrants hidden aboard this merchant vessel.

Coast Guard's role in securing home waters and ports as crucial. Merchant shipping, petroleum tankers, passenger ships, and other types of commercial vessels became the focus of heightened regulations the Coast Guard is charged with enforcing. By boarding vessels to verify information on a ship's **manifest** and by inspecting cargo holds and containers, the Coast Guard is often on the front line of homeland security, helping to keep out illegal migrants and dangerous materials.

Coast Guard Technology

Supporting military operations and handling the complex challenge of enforcing international maritime regulations, in addition to the demands of law enforcement missions, has strained the resources of the Coast Guard.

The service's leaders have expressed concern that older equipment, vessels, and airplanes are not adequate to meet new demands.

Beginning in the 1990s, the Coast Guard studied how the service's technology (particularly its 93 deep-water cutters and more than 200 aircraft) could be made more modern. The Coast Guard approved an $11-billion plan in June 2002, called the Integrated Deepwater Systems program, to replace the fleet of cutters and aircraft, an effort that may take 30 years to complete. The Deepwater program includes buying more than 90 cutters, 35 airplanes, and 34 helicopters, as well as advanced new technologies, such as robot aircraft, to help extend surveillance ranges. A snapshot of the Coast Guard's current inventory includes armed high-endurance cutters, which can move at a maximum speed of 29 knots (33 miles per hour). Coast Guard aviators fly a variety of aircraft,

Above: In the battle against narcotics traffic, the U.S. Coast Guard's fleet includes MH-68A Stingray helicopters — armed with a M240 general purpose machine gun and a .50-caliber sniper rifle.

Right: The U.S. Coast
Guard also deploys military
forces overseas, such as
this U.S. Coast Guard crew
member guarding a Coast
Guard cutter at the port
of Umm Qasr, Iraq, in
July 2003.

ncluding the HC-130H long-range surveillance aircraft and the MH-68A helicopter, armed with a 7.62-mm machine gun and a .50-caliber sniper rifle.

Coast Guard Personnel

To prepare the men and women who will operate and maintain the Coast Guard's cutters and airplanes, the service trains officers and enlisted personnel at two locations. Coast Guard Training Center Cape May, New Jersey, is where enlisted personnel are trained. Officers are trained through the cadet program at the U.S. Coast Guard Academy, New London, Connecticut.

While it is a small service of fewer than 40,000 active-duty members, the Coast Guard has marked some significant firsts in U.S. military history. At the end of the Civil War (1861–1865), President Abraham Lincoln **commissioned** Michael A. Healy, the first African American to receive a commission in the service that would become the Coast Guard. Healy later commanded a cutter, the first time a black officer commanded a federal ship.

Other famous African Americans served in the Coast Guard, perhaps most notably the author Alex Haley, who died in 1992. Haley served in the Coast Guard for 20 years in a variety of assignments, including combat tours in the Pacific during World War II. After leaving the service, Haley wrote *Roots*, a book presenting the legacy of an African family's struggle for freedom, from enslavement in the eighteenth century through the Civil Rights Movement in the United States during the 1960s.

Joining the Coast Guard

Prospective Coast Guard recruits must be United States citizens or nationalized (in order to be officers) and United States citizens or resident aliens (in order to enlist). A new recruit must be between the ages of 17 and 27 and possess a high school diploma. Of approximately 5,500 applicants, an average of 265 students enter the U.S. Coast Guard Academy each year. A Coast Guard recruiting office can be located by phone at **1-877-669-8724.** Additional literature about the Coast Guard can be obtained by calling **1-800-424-8883.** The official web site of the U.S. Coast Guard is **www.uscg.mil.**

Chapter 3
Law Enforcement and Homeland Security

Right: U.S. Navy and U.S. Secret Service boats escort a launch carrying the president during an official overseas visit. Protecting the U.S. government's senior leaders is a key mission for the Secret Service.

Federal law enforcement agencies, such as the Secret Service, help to prevent crimes that may destabilize or erode national security. Before being absorbed by the Department of Homeland Security in 2003, the Secret Service had been part of the Department of the Treasury. The Secret Service was founded at the end of the Civil War in 1865 with a twofold mission. The service is responsible for protecting the president of the United States and the vice president, their families, and other important government officials and their families. Secret Service agents also provide protection for visiting government leaders from other countries.

The Secret Service also investigates financial fraud and counterfeit money offenses, which may contribute to the threat from terrorism by helping to fund terrorists' training and supplies. The government believes terrorists use illegal means of raising money to help finance their attack plans. After the attacks on September 11, 2001, a number of arrests of suspected al-Qaeda members were made based on evidence that terrorist cells in Europe and the United States had raised money to fund the attacks.

The Secret Service also manages the National Threat Assessment Center, which is part of the intelligence capability of the U.S. government, helping to provide information for the Department of Homeland Security concerning the threat of possible terrorist attacks. The Department of Homeland Security publishes a color-coded report from the Homeland Security Advisory System, which ranges from green (meaning low risk of terrorist attack) to red (meaning severe risk of terrorist attack). On average, since September 11, 2001, the threat advisory has remained yellow, meaning there is "significant risk" of a terrorist attack. Some observers of the color-coded advisory system have criticized its use, especially because it does not usually provide specific details about the nature of a threat or what members of the public should do about it.

Below: The Department of Homeland Security has promoted a color-coded threat advisory system. Critics of the system (shown here as depicted on the Internet) have questioned whether it provides enough information to inform the public fully.

The Customs Service

Another law enforcement organization within the Department of Homeland Security is the Customs Service, which had also originally been part of the Department of the Treasury. The Customs Service is now part of the Department of Homeland

Right: A major problem for the U.S. Department of Homeland Security is monitoring more than seven million cargo containers passing through U.S. ports annually.

Security's Border and Transportation Security Directorate. The Customs Service was founded in 1789, and for more than 100 years provided all of the U.S. government's operating funds, mostly by enforcing **tariffs** on goods imported from other countries.

Today, the Border and Transportation Security Directorate helps to improve national security by inspecting cargo and persons traveling across U.S. borders including sea ports, airports, and highway crossings. One objective of the Border and Transportation Security Directorate is to identify and intercept hazardous cargo and illegal migrants before they reach a border checkpoint. That objective requires cooperation with military forces, such as the Coast Guard and the Navy, and with other nations' governments.

The U.S. government and commercial industry are developing technologies to help the identification and interception of potentially hazardous cargo (items such as dangerous chemicals, weapons, and illegal drugs). For example, devices that use high-frequency sound waves to penetrate and identify materials inside containers, without the containers having to be opened, have been deployed aboard Coast Guard vessels patrolling in territorial waters as well as out into the United States' 200 nautical mile range exclusive economic zone. Other

chnologies, including X-ray and gamma ray emitters, are used to scan cargo
r hazardous material before these cross borders. But the task is huge. Of the
llions of dollars worth of cargo that enters the United States everyday, mostly
the form of shipping containers at seaports, not much more than 2 percent
3 percent is actually inspected, according to Senator Dianne Feinstein, a
emocrat from California.

Technologies can only be successful if workable policies are in place that guide
hen, where, and how these limited resources should be used. The United States
nd other countries are developing international regulations that would require
rict accounting of the cargo carried aboard a nation's commercial shipping.
order control officials and the military could query this account, while the cargo
as in transit. For example, a ship approaching the United States without a cargo
port in an internationally approved format could be intercepted, boarded, and
spected well away from a port. Ships that have proper reports would be passed
rough the patrol zone and may then be subjected to inspection by border or port
curity officials. A system that operated in this way would stop and search only
ose vessels approaching U.S. territory which presented the greatest perceived
reat by having no legitimate account of their cargo.

Left: On an average day,
Coast Guard boarding
parties seize almost $10
million worth of illegal
drugs and interdict more
than a dozen illegal
migrants.

Right: The Federal Bureau of Investigation often leads the collection of evidence at the scene of terrorist attacks, such as at the Pentagon on September 11, 2001.

The contributions of federal law enforcement agencies to homeland security aren't all made within the Department of Homeland Security, however. The Department of Justice administers two other policing agencies important to homeland security: the FBI and the DEA.

The Federal Bureau of Investigation (FBI)

In 1908, U.S. Attorney General Charles Bonaparte formed the FBI as an office to provide investigative services for the federal government. During the era of the Great Depression, from 1929 through the 1930s, the FBI broadened its mission to battle organized crime, and later strengthened the role it played in protecting he United States from espionage and **sabotage** by foreign agents. For example, during the 1920s, 1930s, and 1940s—as Italy, Germany, Spain, and apan embraced fascist governments (governments ruled by dictators using military and police force, rather than by a democratic process), and as the communist regime of the Soviet Union expanded its influence during the same era—the FBI was given the task of tracking sympathetic movements within the United States. Some of these "subversive" groups were feared to be the source of possible espionage and sabotage as World War II ignited. When war spread across Europe in the late 1930s and early 1940s with Nazi Germany's invasion of much of Europe and Russia, the FBI focused its internal security efforts on potentially dangerous German, Italian, and apanese nationals as well as native-born Americans whose beliefs and activities were thought to aid America's enemies.

After Japan attacked Pearl Harbor Naval Station, Hawaii, on December 7, 941, bringing the United States into World War II, the U.S. government enacted a policy prohibiting Japanese Americans from living on the West Coast of the United States. This policy led to the forced movement and internment of many Japanese Americans, including persons born in the United States and otherwise demonstrating loyal citizenship. Many people now view the internment policy as a serious violation of human rights, but at the time it was enforced because of widespread fears of spies and saboteurs.

Inarguably, however, the FBI and other government law enforcement branches did succeed in preventing acts of sabotage by foreign agents during World War II. For example, in June 1942, German agents launched a mission against the United States. The German agents had been trained to dress, speak, and behave as Americans in order to blend into society. The Nazi agents were deployed from a submarine off the East Coast of the United States and came ashore in New York and Florida. The German agents had planned to use explosives to destroy industrial facilities, but their plot was foiled when one of the saboteurs surrendered.

The FBI in 2002 restructured its mission focus to emphasize "the prevention of terrorist attacks, on countering foreign intelligence operations against the United States, and on addressing cybercrime-based attacks and other high-technology crimes," according to the Department of Justice.

Above: A U.S soldier guards Japanese Americans interred during World War II. In 1988, President Ronald Reagan offered a presidential apology and compensation to Japanese Americans discriminated against by the federal government.

Civil Liberties

As the lines have blurred between criminal investigations and intelligence gathering in the war against global terrorism, the U.S. government and the governments of other democratic nations face challenges in protecting citizens' civil liberties while still keeping the public safe. The forced internment of Japanese Americans during the 1940s is a reminder to some of the potential for law enforcement and homeland security measures to be taken to an extreme. Today, many Arab Americans and other ethnic groups in the United States who share an Islamic religious and cultural heritage are concerned about the public perception of Muslims since Islamic extremists vocally supported the deadly attacks of September 11, 2001. The U.S. Census Bureau is not tasked with collecting information on residents' religious

The Drug Enforcement Agency

Another agency within the Department of Justice that is part of the United States' homeland security force is the DEA, formed in 1973 as a centralized organization for the investigation of narcotics-related crime. Although combating organized drug trafficking costs millions of dollars and other national resources, the link between drug dealing and international terrorism has been recently emphasized by the Department of Justice. "Not only does [illegal drug trafficking] weaken the United States, but it also supports attacks against the judicial system in Mexico. It funds terrorism in Colombia and generally destabilizes governments from Afghanistan to Thailand," DEA director Asa Hutchinson said in 2002. When the United States and its allies ousted the Taliban regime from Afghanistan, the forces found a still-thriving opium and heroin trade that may have funded al-Qaeda's activities.

Left: The Drug Enforcement Agency combats narcotics trafficking, which the U.S. government believes helps fund terrorist organizations. Here, DEA agents arrest a prominent member of a Colombian cocaine-smuggling cartel.

background, though the bureau quotes as "widely accepted" the figure of between six million and seven million Muslims living in the United States.

The Department of Justice and Congress, under the *U.S.A. Patriot Act of 2001*, condemned discrimination against Arab and Muslim Americans and called for strengthened funding and administrative support to counterterrorism efforts.

On March 25, 2003, Dr. Malik Hasan, of the U.S. delegation to the United Nations' Commission on Human Rights, reported on the problem of discrimination against Muslims living in the United States. Hasan said the U.S. government found no evidence of a "wave" of attacks on Muslims and persons of Arab descent in the United States after September 11, 2001. But Hasan noted "an increase in hate crimes against Arabs, Muslims and Sikhs after the September 11 terrorist attacks. The rate of those offenses then dropped precipitously within a few weeks until, as of mid-January, 2002, the rate had nearly returned to the previously low [level]."

Below: Since the events of September 11, 2001, the government has faced the challenge of protecting civil liberties for more than six million American Muslims against the risk of anti-Islamic prejudice.

Illustrating the senseless nature of hate crimes, since September 11, 2001, press reports emerged of violence committed against Sikhs and Hindus, two religious groups that originate in India and are wholly unconnected with Islam in general and particularly with the kind of Islam professed by groups like al-Qaeda.

The FBI has opened more than 500 investigations into alleged hate crimes against Muslims, ethnic Arabs, and people of East Indian, Pakistani, or other South Asian descent. More than a dozen federal prosecutions and nearly 100 state and local government prosecutions have begun in cases where there was evidence of ethnic discrimination that was perceived to be related to outrage at the September 11, 2001, terrorist attacks.

The U.S. military and other government organizations have been criticized for a policy of arresting non-citizens who for various reasons the government suspects may be associated with terrorist groups. That policy has led to the detainment of nearly 800 persons by the Immigration and Naturalization Service, for example. Of those arrested, most have been sent back to their home countries. At U.S. Naval Base Guantanamo Bay, Cuba, the military has for more than two years held more than 600 people who have been captured in fighting overseas, or

Left: U.S. ethnic and religious minorities, such as Sikhs, have been concerned by possible discrimination in the wake of war in Southwest Asia and the terrorist attacks of 2001.

have been arrested as terrorists. Most of these prisoners are Muslims of various ethnic backgrounds. The international civil rights advocacy group, Human Rights Watch, has criticized the detainment of individuals without trial at Guantanamo Bay.

Joining Federal Law Enforcement Agencies

The federal law enforcement agencies involved in homeland security advertise job vacancies at the Internet site www.usajobs.opm.gov. Federal law enforcement agencies each have their own hiring standards, but generally follow a similar set of requirements. For example, the U.S. Secret Service requires applicants be United States citizens between the ages of 21–37, and to have earned a degree from an accredited four-year college or university. Most law enforcement agencies require applicants to demonstrate excellent health and physical conditioning and have the academic skills to pass an examination set by the specific agency. New federal agents attend 11 weeks of intensive training at the Federal Law Enforcement Training Center at Glynco, Georgia, or at Artesia, New Mexico.

Chapter 4
Emergency Readiness

Right: The Federal Emergency Management Agency works to prepare for and recover from natural disasters—such as this forest fire in New Mexico—as well as man-made tragedies such as acts of terrorism.

The Department of Homeland Security in 2003 formed an Emergency Preparedness and Response Directorate that includes the Federal Emergency Management Agency (FEMA), the U.S. government's most prominent office for disaster preparedness. An important goal for the directorate is better coordination for federal disaster response in the future and to help each state and local "first responders," such as fire departments, emergency medical services, and police, who proved crucial to the recovery from the September 11, 2001, attacks.

President Jimmy Carter in 1979 signed an executive order creating FEMA, which evolved from other organizations whose responsibilities included preparing for natural disasters, as well as developing plans for surviving nuclear war. The agency was responsible for coordinating plans for civil defense and the evacuation of important government workers in the event of a major attack on the United States. During the Cold War era, many Americans feared such an attack by the Soviet Union. FEMA's role now includes helping communities prepare for the possibility of terrorist attacks.

Below: *Bacillus anthracis* is a naturally occurring bacterium that can be harnessed as a weapon to cause the deadly disease anthrax.

Weapons of Mass Destruction

One of the biggest challenges for public-safety planners is building a strategy to respond to attacks by WMD, such as anthrax, a potentially deadly disease caused by bacteria that bear spores. Such spores were found in parcels mailed to postal facilities and government offices in Washington, D.C., and Virginia, and to media offices and postal facilities in the states of Connecticut, Florida, Missouri, New Jersey, New York, and Washington. According to a statement made on October 16, 2003, by Senator Patrick Leahy of Vermont, between September 22, 2001, and November 14, 2001, 11 people were infected with cutaneous or skin anthrax, and 11 contracted the more serious form of the disease, called inhalation or pulmonary anthrax. Five of the victims died, and the attacks led to the U.S. Postal Service

implementing costly decontamination processes and technologies. The threat of additional biological or chemical weapons attacks has raised concerns, particularly about how local hospitals and rescue personnel could be equipped to respond to an area's contamination by highly infectious diseases or deadly toxins, such as those that attack the nervous system.

The use of chemical or biological weaponry in warfare is not a new concept. Some sources credit the use of smallpox in the eighteenth and nineteenth centuries as one of the earliest examples of the intentional use of disease as a weapon. According to a citation in the *Journal of the American Medical Association*, the deadly smallpox virus may have been used as a weapon by British forces against Native peoples in North America in the 1700s.

According to a report from the U.S. Air Force Epidemiology and Public Health Department and the Operational Medicine Division, U.S. Army Medical Research Institute of Infectious Diseases, Fort Detrick, Maryland: "The availability of biological warfare agents and supporting technologic infrastructure, coupled with the fact that there are many people motivated to do harm to the United States, means that America must be prepared to defend her homeland against biological agents."

The Air Force and Army report, from the May 2002 edition of *Emergency Medicine Clinics of North America*, argued that despite the technologic challenge of "isolating, growing, purifying, weaponizing, and disseminating" lethal biological agents, the threat of this technology falling into the hands of terrorists is real. The globalization of biotechnology has forced the United States to accelerate its programs of defense against biological weapons, including the development of pharmaceutical stockpiles (for treating infections by anthrax and other agents), heightened surveillance systems, new vaccine development, and advanced training programs to prepare people how best to respond to different forms of biological attack.

In addition to biological weapons, potential threats from lethal chemical agents have evolved. During World War I, Germany and its opponents (chiefly Great Britain and France) used mustard gas, which is a chemical blister agent, and other agents in artillery shells. Gas weapons damaged mucous membranes in the eyes and throats of victims, resulting in disfigurement, maiming, and death; such weapons are still in use in some countries. That chemical weapons may become

Left: The Centers for Disease Control and Prevention, headquartered at Atlanta, Georgia, is the U.S. government's focal point for implementing environmental health and disease control policies.

tools for terrorism has been demonstrated by the 1995 attack on the Tokyo underground. Members of a group called Aum Shinrikyo released the nerve agent sarin on the Tokyo subway, which transports millions of people every day. Among Aum Shinrikyo's objectives was to shun the modern secular world and bring about, through violence if necessary, the establishment of a **utopia**, a perfect society that renounced spiritual corruption. Aum's attacks left 11 people dead and more than 5,000 injured, raising the alarm about the sort of public destruction that could be wrought with chemical weapons. The cult, renamed Aleph in 2000, continues to practice its beliefs in Japan.

Other types of WMD may also be available to terrorist groups if they have adequate money and support. The U.S. government's intelligence community believes that nuclear weapons, while expensive to develop and as difficult to handle, if not more so, than chemical or biological weapons, could fall into the hands of terrorists. The U.S. government is also concerned that terrorists may use "dirty bombs" in an attack. A dirty bomb is a weapon that uses ordinary explosives to spread radioactive material without requiring the sophisticated engineering of a military nuclear weapon.

As the September 11, 2001, attacks showed, terrorists may make use of "asymmetric" (meaning dissimilar) capabilities to overcome the technological advantage of a powerful military. Civilian airliners were not thought of as potential weapons until the events of September 11, 2001. Military and intelligence analysts view the use of WMD as providing the ultimate asymmetric advantage: forms of attack, defenses against which may easily be overwhelmed. The threats posed by such attacks have prompted public officials to reassess the ways in which federal, state, and local leaders prepare for and respond to terrorism. For example, the Department of Homeland Security manages the Homeland Security Advisory System to publicize the federal government's assessment of the threat from

Below: In 1995, the religious sect Aum Shinrikyo used the nerve agent sarin to attack a Tokyo subway.

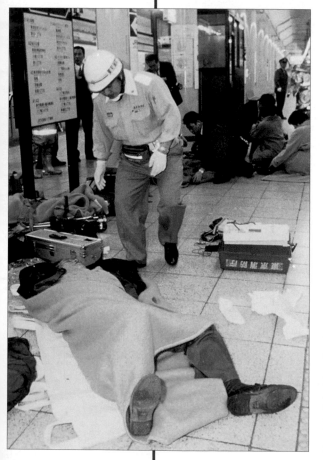

errorist attacks; DHS also created a cyber security office to manage the effort to protect computer networks that control critical infrastructure, such as electrical power, water, and transportation computer networks. Additionally, the Department of Homeland Security has backed a community emergency response team (CERT) program, which was developed from a Los Angeles, California, fire department training program. The CERT program, which FEMA has promoted nationwide, provides community officials with training in disaster response preparation, basic medical treatment skills, search and rescue, and team cooperation with other federal, state, and local agencies.

Above: State and local rescue workers, such as these New York City firefighters, were on the front line following the September 11, 2001, terrorist attacks.

Chapter 5
The Military and Homeland Defense

Right: An F/A-18 Hornet is prepared for launch from the flight deck of USS *George Washington* in the Atlantic Ocean on September 15, 2001. Carrier-based fighter aircraft patrolled the skies over New York City in the aftermath of the September 11 attacks.

Military forces have roles to play in homeland security and defense, but the Posse Comitatus Act, which prohibits the Department of Defense from directly enforcing laws, limits these roles. *Posse comitatus* is a Latin phrase meaning "power, or force, of the state." The law passed in June 1878 reads:

It shall not be lawful to employ any part of the Army of the United States, as a posse comitatus, or otherwise, for the purpose of executing the laws, except in such cases and under such circumstances as such employment of said force may be expressly authorized by the Constitution or by Act of Congress.

While this law limits the range of operations the military may undertake within U.S. territory, the Department of Defense does contribute to both homeland defense and security.

Homeland Security and Homeland Defense

The military defines homeland security and homeland defense as separate ideas. For military forces, homeland security means "the prevention…and defense against, aggression targeted at U.S. territory, sovereignty, domestic population, and infrastructure, as well as the

Below: The U.S. military is now looking outward in its mission of defense. New organizations like Northern Command now bridge the missions of the Department of Defense with those of Homeland Security.

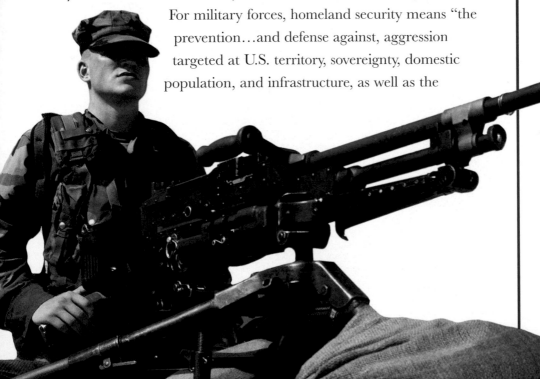

Above: Soldiers of the U.S. Army National Guard help fight wildfires in Montana.

management of the consequences of such aggression and other domestic emergencies," according to a Pentagon administered web site, www.northcom.mil. The Department of Homeland Security takes the lead in matters of internal security, with the military playing a supporting role. The www.northcom.mil site defines homeland defense as "the protection of U.S. territory, domestic population, and critical infrastructure against military attacks emanating from outside the United States." Defending, from a military standpoint, means taking the fight to where the enemy resides, such as was the case during Operation Enduring Freedom in 2001 and 2002, when U.S. and allied military forces led a campaign thousands of miles from the United States in Afghanistan against al-Qaeda and the then-ruling Taliban regime, which was believed to support al-Qaeda and offer Afghanistan as a base for al-Qaeda attacks.

North American Aerospace Defense Command

Regular military forces have prepared powerful tools for homeland defense. During the Cold War, the military prepared to respond to a possible all-out nuclear attack from enemy bomber planes and ballistic missiles. One of the ways in which the military planned its response was the formation of the North American Aerospace Defense Command (NORAD), a cooperative effort between the U.S. and Canadian militaries that dates back to 1958. NORAD, with its fortress-like command-and-control center deep within Cheyenne Mountain Air Force Station, Colorado, has had a primary mission of defending against threats coming from outside the borders of the United States and Canada. After September 11, 2001, however, NORAD's mission changed. Today, the command is responsible for domestic airspace defense as well.

The Canadian and United States governments have a cooperative agreement giving NORAD the authority to exercise its influence in several regions. In the Alaskan defense region, airplanes and radar systems are on alert to detect incoming airplanes or **cruise missiles**, as are the forces of the Canadian defense region. At Tyndall U.S. Air Force Base, Florida, the First Air Force (a unit made up entirely of Air National Guardsmen) is the primary combat resource for defending the airspace of the American homeland. First Air Force also helps the Coast Guard, other agencies, and allies hunt down illegal drug traffickers.

U.S. Northern Command

One of the ways the military has tried to improve partnerships with other agencies for separate defense and security missions is by founding a new command organization, called the U.S. Northern Command, which has its headquarters at Peterson Air Force Base, Colorado. This location, in the shadow of NORAD's Cheyenne Mountain command complex, puts Northern Command at the center of a network of surveillance-satellite control stations, air bases, and naval and land forces, providing information and deterrence. The military's concept of defense relies heavily on a strong deterrence, meaning showing others that the United States possesses the ability to retaliate against any attack, in hope of an aggressive person, group, or nation reconsidering the use of violence.

Above: The U.S. Northern Command is the newest of the military's nine "combatant commands," with authority for missions in and around the United States.

Northern Command is considered one of the Department of Defense's "combatant commands," with the ability to call up and command military units during operations within its geographic area of control, which includes U.S. territory in North America, and the air, land, and sea approaches (about 500 miles out from shore) to the continental United States, Alaska, Canada, and Mexico. The military forces upon which Northern Command could call in a crisis include the Marine Corps' Chemical/Biological Incident Response Force (CBIRF). The CBIRF, which is headquartered at Marine Corps Base Quantico, Virginia, is a specially equipped unit of Marines trained to operate in an area contaminated by chemical or biological agents. The CBIRF routinely trains with civil authorities to give and take lessons on how to respond in a crisis. For example, the CBIRF in October 2003 trained with the New York City fire department in search and rescue, decontamination, and crisis management techniques.

Other capabilities the Northern Command has at its disposal include powerful disaster recovery equipment that would be too expensive for many state and local governments to keep on hand. For example, in November 2003, as wildfire raged in the western United States, Northern Command sent into action many of its Air Force, Air National Guard, Air Force Reserve, Navy, and Marine Corps aircraft squadrons, with C-130 transport planes and CH-53 heavy lift helicopters, specially equipped to fight fire.

The National Guards

The Army National Guard and the Air Force Air National Guard are not part of the Department of Homeland Security. The Guards are defense forces at the ready for use by state and federal governments. Nevertheless, these military organizations, more than any others, are responsible for action that is directly related to securing and defending the American homeland. The Guard forces have, for many years, provided equipment, people, and training for homeland defense and homeland security missions. The Air National Guard is considered a "reserve component" of the Air Force, with pilots and ground crew in the

Guard training to the same standards as their counterparts in the "active component" Air Force. A similar relationship exists between the U.S. Army and the Army National Guard.

The Army National Guard

The Army National Guard has evolved from the "citizen soldiers" who formed the first colonial, and later state, militias in North America. Militia units made up a significant number of the land force available to the Continental military during the Revolutionary War. Colonial militias had been on the front lines of combat during the previous century as British settlements established footholds in North America. When the British and French governments fought in the French and Indian War (1754–1763) over control of colonial territories in eastern North America, militia units were relied upon. George Washington,

Above: U.S. Air Force Air National Guard security troops and others from the military's reserve component have been closely integrated with active duty forces carrying out missions at home and abroad.

Right: National Guard troops patrolled civilian and government facilities in the aftermath of the September 11, 2001, terrorist attacks. Here Idaho government officials meet with a member of the National Guard on guard duty at Boise Air Terminal during October 2001.

who became the commander-in-chief of Continental forces during the Revolutionary War, was an officer in the Virginia colonial militia.

When mobilized, the soldiers of the Army National Guard may be under the authority of the Department of Defense. Soldiers in the Army National Guard usually serve one weekend per month and two weeks of annual training when not mobilized. Those soldiers who are called up and mobilized for overseas missions or other tasks may serve longer periods on active duty. In addition to service for the federal government, the Army National Guard is at the disposal of a state or territory's governor, who can call up men and women of the National Guard to help deal with a crisis. Army National Guard forces have been used to help respond to forest fires, earthquakes, and civil disruptions, such as riots. An important example of the use of Army National Guard troops for peacekeeping came in the 1950s and 1960s, during the Civil Rights Movement. The Army National Guard helped to enforce the transition from a segregated society of black and white to one that included integrated schools and integrated public transportation.

Across the country, following the 2001 terrorist attacks, the Army National Guard helped to increase security at airports and other transportation hubs.

or the first time in many years, armed soldiers patrolled civilian areas to heighten security and to provide highly visible reassurance to the public. The Army National Guard has also been ordered to help develop rapid-response capability against future attacks from terrorists using weapons of mass destruction.

The Air National Guard

The Air National Guard has built upon its history to make a significant contribution to homeland defense and homeland security. Before the U.S. Air Force became an independent service, breaking away from the Army in 1947, National Guard forces included almost 30 aviation squadrons. When the first big test of the new U.S. Air Force happened during the Korean War (1950–1953), the Air National Guard was part of that effort, flying almost 40,000 combat sorties with its bomber and fighter planes. During the Korean War, in which North Korea invaded South Korea, the United States was part of a United Nations (U.N.)-supported mission to defend South Korea and drive back the North Koreans.

The U.S. Air Force and the Air National Guard have worked out a cooperative relationship in which there is mutual support and teamwork. During Operation

Left: An important factor in the success of active duty and reserve force integration is standardized training, like this exercise taking place at the small-arms range at the U.S. Army facility in Fort Smith, Arkansas.

Desert Shield/Desert Storm (1990–1991), more than 5,000 Air National Guard troops went overseas to fly air refueling, reconnaissance, airlift, and special forces missions. Air National Guard special forces missions included flying psychological operations missions with specially equipped EC-130 aircraft, transmitting "surrender appeals" and other information to hostile forces during Operation Desert Storm in 1991. The war had begun after the small, oil-rich Middle Eastern nation Kuwait had been invaded by its larger neighbor Iraq under the dictatorship of Saddam Hussein. Cooperation between Air Force and Air National Guard units also means that Air Guard squadrons contribute to all of the United States' air defense interceptor capability. For example, Air National Guard F-15 fighter jets patrolled the skies over U.S. cities after September 11, 2001.

Looking to the Future

As the military and law enforcement agencies involved in the defense and security of the United States look to the future, their focus is on being ready for the next possible crisis or attack. Well before the disasters of September 11, 2001, the government had considered the complex problem of integrating military, law enforcement, and emergency response capabilities. In 2000, Secretary of Defense William S. Cohen spoke about the threat posed by terrorist attacks with weapons of mass destruction in possibly overwhelming state and local emergency response systems. He said the Department of Defense

Exceptions to the *Posse Comitatus* Act

Congress has allowed some exceptions to the regulations prohibiting military forces from enforcing U.S. laws. The military may assist civil law enforcement organizations, such as is now common in the anti-narcotic trafficking operations around the Gulf of Mexico and along the Southwest border area of the United States. Additionally, during a civil disturbance the president may allow states to use regular military forces, along with the Army National Guard, to help restore and keep order. Other emergency situations, such as terrorist bombings, may result in the use of federal military forces to back up first responders.

ncreasingly would be called upon to help, and that the tension between laws designed to protect civil liberties from abuse by military or other government orces would have to be weighed against the risks from a major attack. The Department of Homeland Security, working with the military and other federal and state organizations, has set out to break down some of the barriers to cooperation among agencies. With the risks to life and property now clear after the attacks in New York, Washington, D.C., and Pennsylvania, the government has set a goal of defending against terrorism by disrupting attacks as they are being planned so that they never have the opportunity to succeed. In the process of making these preparations, America's homeland defense and homeland security forces also must prepare to deal with other crises, such as natural disasters, civil unrest, and war.

Above: Personnel such as this Air Force pilot continue to play important roles in homeland defense and security missions.

Time Line

17th century: The first North American colonial militias, forerunners of the National Guard, are formed.

1775–1783: Militia forces fight in the Revolutionary War.

1865: July 5, the U.S. Secret Service is established.

1908: The Federal Bureau of Investigation (FBI) is created.

1915: January 28, President Woodrow Wilson approves the U.S. Coast Guard.

1941–1945: The U.S. Coast Guard fights in World War II.

1947: The Air Force Air National Guard is established.

1958: North American Aerospace Defense Command (NORAD) is established.

1973: The Drug Enforcement Agency (DEA) is created.

1979: The Federal Emergency Management Agency (FEMA) is created.

2001: September 11, terrorist attacks kill 3,028 people in the United States; September 20, the president proposes a Department of Homeland Security; October 7, Operation Enduring Freedom, the war against the Taliban and al-Qaeda in Afghanistan, begins; October 8, President George W. Bush establishes a preliminary office for homeland security and appoints former Pennsylvania Governor Tom Ridge as its director.

2002: January 1, the Department of Homeland Security (DHS) is established; January 7, Congress establishes the Select Committee on Homeland Security with oversight of DHS funding and activity; January 17, the Taliban Regime in Afghanistan is overthrown and the U.S. Embassy, which had been closed for more than 25 years, is reopened; January 24, Tom Ridge is officially sworn in as the Secretary of Homeland Security; October 1, the Pentagon establishes the new U.S. Northern Command.

Glossary

assassination:	a murder by sudden or secret attack usually for impersonal reasons
caliphate:	the office of a successor of Muhammad as temporal and spiritual head of Islam
commission:	to grant military rank or authority
contraband:	goods or merchandise whose importation, exportation, or possession is forbidden
cruise missile:	a long-range missile that can be launched from a ship, airplane, or ground vehicle, seeking targets using a pre-programmed guidance system
fundamentalist:	describing a movement or attitude stressing strict and literal adherence to a set of basic principles; someone who believes in such adherence
infrastructure:	the system of public works of a country, state, or region
internment:	the act of confining or impounding, especially during a war
manifest:	a list of passengers or an invoice of cargo for a vehicle
nationalist:	a person who advocates national independence from outside influences and promotes national cultures and interests
sabotage:	destructive or obstructive action carried on by a civilian or enemy agent to hinder a nation's war effort
tariff:	a fee imposed by a government on imported, or in some countries exported, goods
territorial waters:	waters under the jurisdiction of a nation or state; according to the United Nations' Law of the Sea Treaty, 1994, territorial waters extend 12 nautical miles (more than 13 miles or 22 kilometers) from a country's shore.
utopia:	an idealized place or state of perfection

Further Information

Books:

Corona, Laurel. *Hunting Down the Terrorists: Declaring War and Policing Global Violations.* San Diego: Lucent Books, 2003.

Keeley, Jennifer. *Deterring & Investigating Attacks: The Role of the FBI & CIA.* San Diego: Lucent Books, 2003.

Kerrigan, Michael. *Department of Homeland Security.* Philadelphia: Mason Crest Publishers, 2003.

Sanna, Ellyn. *Homeland Security Officer.* Philadelphia: Mason Crest Publishers, 2003.

Torr, James D. *Responding to Attack: Firefighters and Police.* San Diego: Lucent Books, 2003.

Web sites:

The U.S. Coast Guard

www.uscg.mil/

This site presents the history, present operations, and future plans of the U.S. Coast Guard.

The U.S. Department of Defense

www.defenselink.mil/

This site provides information and links to the United States' armed forces online.

The U.S. Department of Homeland Security

www.dhs.gov/dhspublic/

This is the homepage for the DHS, including links to subordinate organizations, such as the Secret Service and FEMA.

The Federal Bureau of Investigation

www.fbi.gov/

This is the homepage for the FBI, hosted by the Department of Justice.

The U.S. National Guard Bureau

www.ngb.army.mil/

This web site provides history, missions, and outlook for the National Guard, including links to the Air National Guard.

Index